BLACK GIRL

A PLAY IN TWO ACTS
BY J.E. FRANKLIN

★

★

DRAMATISTS
PLAY SERVICE
INC.

SPECIAL NOTE

BLACK GIRL was presented by the Henry Street Settlement's New Federal Theatre (Woodie King and Dick Williams) at the Theatre de Lys, in New York City, on June 16, 1971. It was directed by Shauneille Perry; the setting was by Charles Mills; costumes were by Femi; and the lighting by Buddy. The presentation was by special arrangement with Lucille Lortel Productions, Inc. The cast, in order of appearance, was as follows:

BILLIE JEAN .... Kishasa

LITTLE EARL .... Arthur W. French III

SHERYL .... Robbin Dunn, Jerle Moore, Lorraine Ryder
(alternating performances)

NORMA .... Gloria Edwards

RUTH ANN .... Loretta Greene

MAMA ROSIE .... Louise Stubbs

MU'DEAR .... Minnie Gentry

MR. HERBERT .... Jimmy Hayeson

EARL .... Arthur French

NETTA .... Saundra Sharp

TIME: Present

PLACE: A small town in Texas

(The play was performed without intermission)

3

BLACK GIRL

ACT I

Scene 1

The scene is the living room, where Norma, around twenty-one, and Ruth Ann, aged twenty, are present. Norma is sitting in the big arm chair, her head propped up on her elbow. Her shoes are kicked off and there is a dejected, apathetic expression on her face. Norma is slightly over-weight and seems conscious of it. Her blouse is hanging outside her skirt, and from time to time she tugs at the blouse to cover a part of her stomach.

Two small children are also in the room. One is Norma's little girl, Sheryl, aged four. The other is Ruth Ann's son, aged five. Sheryl is trying to climb up on her mother, while Earl plays on the floor with a toy.

Ruth Ann is setting up the ironing board to prepare for ironing.

The furniture in this room is of the "department-store window" type, unimaginative and failing in its attempt to look classy . . . and one is almost acutely aware of the attempt. Ruffled doilies, stiff with starch and smoothly ironed, are on the arms and backs of the armchair and couch. A well-polished coffee table, bearing an artificial plant, seems to be in the room only because it "goes with the set." On top of the television set is a photo of a young girl in a high school cap and gown. Hanging over the T.V. set is an amateurish water-color reproduction of Jesus praying in the Garden of Gethsemane.

Billie Jean enters the living room. She is a young girl of nearly eighteen . . . dressed in sneakers and a blouse which hangs, in the manner of a tomboy, outside her dungarees. She is holding a cracked LP record in her hands.

BILLIE JEAN. Norma, I asked you and Ruth Ann to please keep them children out-a my room . . . now, they done broke my records.

EARL. I didn't do that, mama.

SHERYL. Me, neither, Mama.

BILLIE JEAN. (*Unable to control herself.*) Well, it didn't break itself!

NORMA. Girl, don't be hollering at these children . . . they said they didn't break the damn record.

BILLIE JEAN. Yeah, like they said they didn't tear the picture of that dancer off-a my wall. (*Ruth Ann begins to iron . . . a white uniform . . . as if what is going on does not concern her.*)

NORMA. Billie Jean, the way you be kicking your legs all up when you doing that bal'let-dancing stuff . . . you could-a broke it yourself.

BILLIE JEAN. It ain't no bal'let dancing.

NORMA. That's what it look like to me.

BILLIE JEAN. Anyway, the record was inside the cover . . . and mighty funny it just happen to be the very one I was practicing my dancing with . . .

NORMA. These children can't even read. How're they gonna just pick out some record you was dancing to?

BILLIE JEAN. Maybe they had some help.

NORMA. (*Indignant and menacing.*) I know damn well you ain't accusing me of breaking no record.

RUTH ANN. (*Setting the iron aside and swinging around.*) You better not be accusing me. (*Mama Rosie calls from her bedroom.*)

MAMA ROSIE. (*Off stage.*) Y'awl got my uniform ready in there, Ruth Ann?

NORMA. (*Speaking loudly.*) She could have it finished, mama, if Billie Jean would leave her alone.

BILLIE JEAN. (*Intimidated and speaking in a whisper.*) I'm not bothering her.

NORMA. Well, get on out-a here, then. (*Mama Rosie's tall, powerful, attractive form looms in the doorway. The room shrinks before this big, black woman.*)

MAMA ROSIE. What's going on in here?

NORMA. She starting some mess about some old record.

BILLIE JEAN. Mama, somebody broke the record I was practicing my dancing with.

MAMA ROSIE. Girl, I don't wanna hear nothing about no darn dancing . . . I done told you that old mess you doing ain't nothing. What the devil you keep-a carrying on over it for? Talking 'bout practice! You wanna practice on something, practice on trying to follow that child's example . . . (*Mama Rosie has thrust a thumb in the direction of the photo sitting on the T.V. set.*) Hurry up, will ya', Ruth Ann . . .

RUTH ANN. All right. (*Mama Rosie exits from whence she came. Ruth Ann keeps an unconcerned face until Billie Jean, too, exits sullenly . . . Then, as if she could barely hold in the giggling, Ruth Ann lets go, turning around on her tip toes, and kicking out a leg in an exaggerated mocking of Billie's dancing. But Norma does not join in the amusement. She is glaring daggers at the photo on the T.V. set. Impulsively she gets up, goes to the T.V. and gives the photo a back-hand slap, knocking it flat. Ruth Ann interrupts her clowning enough to chime in her approval.*) A-Man!

END OF SCENE 1

ACT I

SCENE 2

The scene is Billie Jean's room. Located in the middle of the house, it represents a freak in architecture. One door of the room leads to the back of the house, the other, in the manner of a railroad flat, leads to the front. In order for one to get from the front of the house to the back, and vice versa, he must pass through Billie Jean's room. She keeps the doors locked, and, whenever she has to unlock the doors to let people through, she shows deep annoyance.

It must have taken quite some maneuvering to get three beds into this room, but they are there. On one side of the room is a pair of bunk beds; on the other side is an old-fashioned bed with cast iron foot and head posts. In one tight corner of the room is a record player. Clothes are hanging from nails that have been hammered into the walls. Record covers and photos of entertainers, especially

7

anyone in a dance pose, are cluttered into the few, precious spots remaining on the walls. The linoleum rug is worn down to the black.

When this scene opens, Billie Jean is dancing to Ahmad Jamal's "Poinciana." The movements of the dance she is performing are graceful and precise, as if she had taken a great deal of time and thought to put this piece together to perform before an audience. Billie Jean's body movements are almost three-dimensional. The dance itself is intricate and very expressive, like her face while she is performing it.

The medium of jazz, the classical and modern, and the raw-primitive can be detected intermingled innocently into one innovation. It is obvious that Billie Jean has a great deal of talent, and, with polish and training it all could develop into something, though God only knows what the innovation would be called now.

In the middle of the dance a timid knock is heard at the door which leads to the front of the house. Billie Jean stops dancing and reacts with annoyance. She turns the music down and goes to unlatch the door. Earl pops through the crack Billie Jean has allowed and runs to the other door, trying to unlatch it. Sheryl, wide-eyed and timid, tries to follow Earl.

BILLIE JEAN. What y'awl want?

LITTLE BOY. We want some water.

BILLIE JEAN. Leave that latch alone, and get out-a my room . . . both of you. (The little girl, frightened, scrambles to the door from whence she came. The boy stays and tries to unlatch the door. Billie Jean goes to wrestle him away.)

LITTLE BOY. I'm gonna tell Big Mama.

BILLIE JEAN. Next time your mama leave you with me, I'm gonna beat your ass.

LITTLE BOY. Mama said tell her next time you beat me.

BILLIE JEAN. So, tell her, with your nappy-head self. And you better not bring your butt back in here. (Billie Jean slams the door, latches it, and is about to turn the record player up again when a loud knock is heard at the same door and a voice is calling, "Billie Jean, open this door, child." Billie Jean's grandmother, whose name,

8

Mu'Dear, is a lazy form of "Mother-dear," will enter. When Mu'Dear, a short, thin woman of fifty-five, gets full into the room, the children will dart through, unlatch the other door, and exit.)

MU'DEAR. Billie Jean, why don't you let these children get their water and stop scaring them all the time?

BILLIE JEAN. I ain't scaring them, Mu'Dear . . . they pass back and forth through my room all day long and they don't be wanting nothing out-a that kitchen.

MU'DEAR. Billie Jean, how do you know they don't want nothing?

BILLIE JEAN. I know they don't be wanting nothing, Mu'Dear. Their mothers put 'em up to running back and forth through here.

MU'DEAR. Billie Jean, what is this mess you keeping up lately about somebody picking on you? You losing your mind locked up in this room every day like this, child.

BILLIE JEAN. Yeah, that's right, Mu'Dear, I'm losing my mind. It's just my imagination that when Norma and Ruth Ann was living here, they kept their things all over the room, and if I didn't keep my stuff hid in boxes under the bed, they'd disappear. They can't stand to see me finally have this room all to myself. That's why they send all those stray girls to live here. But I'm losing my mind 'cause I see through their mess.

MU'DEAR. Oh, yes, Miss Billie Jean, go 'head on make a joke out-a what I say. You won't get far in this world if you disrespect your parents and grandparents . . . God don't like ugly. (*A man enters the room from the door leading to the kitchen. He is about ten years older than Mu'Dear. A short man like she is, he is plump . . . a stub of a cigar stuck between his teeth and a tired expression on his face. Mr. Herbert, trying to look pleasant, speaks to Mu'Dear and Billie as he enters the room.*)

MR. HERBERT. Hey. How y'awl doing?

MU'DEAR. (*Trying to conceal the worry on her face.*) Hey, Herbert. (*He crosses the room, going for the other door.*)

BILLIE JEAN. At least you could-a knocked, Mr. Herbert.

MU'DEAR. (*Angry.*) Now, listen here, Billie Jean, I'm not gonna stand for your mess, child! I'm just not gonna stand for it!

BILLIE JEAN. I wasn't talking to you, Mu'Dear.

MR. HERBERT. What's the trouble here?

MU'DEAR. I'm gonna tell Rosie she better do something with Billie Jean, 'cause I don't play with no children. (*Mu'Dear leaves the room in a huff . . . Mr. Herbert follows, puzzled. Billie Jean*

9

locks the door after them, then lies on her bed, resting herself on her elbows. She watches the door, sullen and defiant. First there is an attempt . . . as if by an angry bull . . . to charge through the barrier. Then we hear the voice of Mama Rosie, commanding: "Open this door, girl!" Billie Jean tries not to show her intimidation, but it is hard to hide the fear.)

MAMA ROSIE. Billie Jean, ain't I told you to keep this door open? Open that other door over yonder!

BILLIE JEAN. *(In a pacifying tone.)* Mama, sometimes I be in here undressing and Mr. Herbert just walk in without even knocking.

MAMA ROSIE. You don't be undressing all them times you keep this door locked. Who you think you talking to? Besides, Mr. Herbert done seen plenty kinds of whatever you trying to hide.

BILLIE JEAN. If Mr. Herbert was married to Mu'Dear, that would be different, Mama, but he ain't no kin to nobody in this house.

MAMA ROSIE. That ain't none-a your business, Billie Jean. And as far as you're concerned, Mr. Herbert is a *roomer* here.

BILLIE JEAN. *(Innocently.)* If he is a roomer, how come he ain't got a room to hisself?

MAMA ROSIE. *(Drawing in air.)* Girl, did you hear me! It ain't-non-a-your-business-who-my-mother-have-in-her-room! You keep your trap shut about it or get out and get you a place of your own! *(Billie Jean takes this without outward emotion, then speaks slowly and calmly in an attempt to hide her hurt.)*

BILLIE JEAN. Might funny when some other girl's mother put her out on the street, mama, you open up your big heart and welcome her in this house. But I gotta get out and . . .

MAMA ROSIE. *(Loudly . . . saving herself from the condemnation.)* Those other girls knows how to be 'preciative and stay in a child's place; and if you're gonna lay up here on your lazy behind all day long, you're gonna stay in a child's place, too, or yes, you *will* get your own place or get you a husband, one! *(The two children pass back through the room. The little boy, catching the meat of this conversation, sticks his tongue out at Billie Jean before tearing from the room.)*

BILLIE JEAN. *(Hissing at him.)* You ugly bastard!

MAMA ROSIE. Billie Jean, you just mean and hateful! Those little babies can't do a thing to you . . . *(Mama Rosie stops abruptly. She can hardly believe that she hears the sound of hum-*

10

ming coming from Billie Jean's direction. She stares menacingly and incredulously at Billie Jean, who, on second thought, finds it too dangerous to try her mother.) Gal, do you want me to get a stick and beat all the black off-a you? You better snap out-a whatever's on your mind, do you hear me? Don't you roll your eyes at me! *(Mama Rosie raps Billie Jean on the head with a fist. Billie flinches and looks pitifully at her mother.)* This ain't 'Deah you playing with!

BILLIE JEAN. I wasn't rolling my eyes at you, mama.

RUTH ANN. *(Pushing into the room . . . hand on hip.)* Billie Jean, what did you call my baby?

BILLIE JEAN. He was sticking his tongue out at me.

RUTH ANN. That don't give you no right to be calling him no bastard . . . a bastard is a child that ain't got no daddy, and *my* baby got a daddy.

MAMA ROSIE. Don't you worry. Billie Jean is getting her tail out-a this house tomorrow and look for her a job. Glued to this room . . .

NORMA. *(Off stage.)* She already got a job, mama! *(Ruth Ann reacts uneasily . . . wants no part of this.)*

MAMA ROSIE. Already got one where?

NORMA. *(Off stage.)* At the Groovey Bar and Grill in Second Ward.

MAMA ROSIE. At the Groovey Bar and Grill! Doing what?!

NORMA. *(Off stage.)* Doin' that bal'let dancing! *(Ruth Ann slowly slides out of the room and disappears.)*

BILLIE JEAN. It ain't no bal'let dancing!

NORMA. *(Off stage, spelling.)* P-a-l-l-e-t is pal'let, ain't it? Well, b-a-l-l-e-t *gots* to be bal'let.

BILLIE JEAN. It ain't even that *kind*-a dancing!

MAMA ROSIE. Never mind what kind-a dancing it is, Billie Jean . . . I wants to hear 'bout this job you supposed to have.

NORMA. *(Off stage.)* Mr. Groovey Grill hired her to do that bal'let dancing!

MAMA ROSIE. Norma Faye, shut up and let me find out what this mess is all about?

BILLIE JEAN. He didn't hire me just to dance, mama . . . I wait on the customers first and when the other girl come on shift, that's when I dance.

MAMA ROSIE. Have you started this mess yet, Billie Jean?

BILLIE JEAN. I just worked three nights.

MAMA ROSIE. How come I'm just now hearing about this?

NORMA. (*Off stage.*) I thought she had told you, mama. It's a job. I didn't see no reason for her to hide no job . . . 'less it's something else she doing.

BILLIE JEAN. I was gonna tell you, mama.

MAMA ROSIE. Oh, you was *gonna* tell me.

BILLIE JEAN. After I got my first week's pay, I was . . .

MAMA ROSIE. Billy Jean, you ain't gonna see no week at *that* place. You *knows* darn well I don't 'prove-a this dancing mess, nohow . . . and shaking your tail in the Groovey Grill of all places! You know I didn't raise none-a y'awl like that.

NORMA. (*Off stage.*) Them guys don't wanna see no bal'let dancing, nohow . . . they wanna see some strip-T. (*Giggles are heard from the living room.*)

MAMA ROSIE. How much is you getting for this mess?

NORMA. (*Off stage.*) $3 a night!

MAMA ROSIE. $3 a night!?

BILLIE JEAN. But I get tips, mama.

MAMA ROSIE. Tip!? I don't care how many tips you get, Billie Jean! Don't you know $3 a night ain't no kind-a salary to be paying nobody? Why, he don't think you worth nothing!

NORMA. (*Off stage.*) You get more than that picking cotton!

MAMA ROSIE. (*Speaking into the living room.*) Norma Faye, y'awl know darn well I didn't know 'bout Billie Jean working for no $3 a night! Y'awl know you should-a came and told me when you first heard about this! Talking 'bout tip! You better tip your ass over there some time today and get what that man owe you and I better not never hear-a you in no place like that again, 'less you got you a husband to take you in one. (*There is nothing but the sound of giggling coming from the living room.*) That truant officer walk in there and you out-a school and under-eighteen, you can get carried right off to reform school and they make *me* pay a fine. (*There is the sound of rumbling in the living room . . . Then Norma rushes to the door of Billie's room and speaks eagerly.*)

NORMA. Mama, daddy just drove up.

MAMA ROSIE. (*Interest flashing across her face.*) You kidding!

NORMA. Naw, I ain't kidding, either. (*Forgetting all about Billie Jean, Mama Rosie, making a motion as if to rush into the living room, harnesses her reflex action and tries to show as little interest*

12

as possible. Once in the living room, she catches a quick glimpse from the window.)

MAMA ROSIE. That jive ass bastard! Don't tell him I'm here. *(She begins to rush into the hallway leading to her bedroom. Once she stops, turns to add something before disappearing.)* Any man stay 'way from me for six years is gonna have ta' go through some changes to see me. *(Ruth Ann is rushing toward the other bedroom to get Mu'Dear and Mr. Herbert. Excitement is high. Billie Jean peeps from her room but does not leave it. She stands at the door, a forlorn, defeated, humiliated look on her face. Earl, Mama Rosie's ex-husband, has just entered the living room. Earl is what might be called a pretty-man, everything about him . . . his clothes, his hair . . . is fixed just so. His hair is processed and shiny like the material of which his suit is made. Not a strand of his hair is lifted, and the suit is pressed so well the creases stand out on his pants. A big man with broad shoulders and a muscular frame, he is a little lighter-skinned than Mama Rosie. Earl has a great deal of presence. He is proud of something about himself and is acutely aware of the storm he is creating. He stands tall and self-confident, plucking arrogantly at the creases of his pants or fingering the rings on his fingers. The two children hug close to their mothers, regarding Earl as if he were a strange being, the likes of which they have never seen before. Norma and Ruth Ann are looking out of the window at the car Earl has just driven up.)*

RUTH ANN. Ooooo, daddy . . . oooo, that is boss! I ain't lying!

NORMA. Man, that thing is talking *my* language!

RUTH ANN. *(Looking proudly at her father.)* Daddy, you shore clean! I mean!

EARL. Aw, you ain't seen nothing yet. I just didn't wanna mess these little old country boys' minds up the first day. *(Mu'Dear and Mr. Herbert appear from the direction of the front bedroom. Mu'Dear and Earl are glad to see each other. The two of them hug . . . Earl making sure to pat his hair back in place after the hug.)*

MU'DEAR. Well, there's my boy! How you doing, son? Lord, you shore looking well.

EARL. Hey, Deah. What's going on, Herbert?

MR. HERBERT. Aw, nothing, Earl . . . you know . . . same old thing . . . working hard.

EARL. Gimme five, man. *(The two men shake hands as if they had*

13

once been enemies, Herbert making every effort to hide the envy in his eyes. He seems humbled and depreciated by the presence of this big, stylish man, who is flaunting his success. Herbert keeps Earl at bay with his eyes.)

RUTH ANN. Come dig this view, Mr. Herbert! *(Herbert and Mu'Dear go to the window to look.)*

EARL. Man, I thought you'd-a been done left this town.

MR. HERBERT. What I wanna leave for if I like it? *(Earl answers with a shrug.)*

MU'DEAR. Well, you shore went and did something for yourself, Earl . . . I'm proud of you. But why don't you come see us more often? You know as far as I'm concerned, you're still a member of this family. Don't you pay no 'tention to Rosie. *(Mama Rosie appears in the doorway and stands unnoticed . . . her hands propped sassily on her hips. She regards Earl, a little contemptuous smile on her face.)*

EARL. *(Blushing.)* Aw, you know I ain't scared-a your daughter, Deah. I'm just a mover . . . you know me.

MU'DEAR. Well, we missed you, Earl. And I saw your mother last week. She was just saying she wished you would come be with her for Mother's Day.

EARL. That's what I'm here for, Deah . . . to see both-a my mothers for Mother's Day.

MU'DEAR. *(Giving him a big hug.)* Well, God bless your heart . . . God bless you, Earl.

EARL. *(Noticing the children.)* Say, whose is them?

RUTH ANN. *(Pointing.)* This one's mine, daddy . . . I named him after you.

MU'DEAR. Didn't your mother write and tell you you had grand-children?

NORMA. Shore, she did, 'cause I was over to Big Mama's the day she wrote the letter.

EARL. But she talked like they was little bitty little ole things.

MU'DEAR. Three years ago they was. Ain't nobody heard nothing from you since then.

EARL. Deah, if I didn't have to hide from these women . . . they all after me.

NORMA. Sheryl, y'awl go hug your grandpa's neck.

EARL. Look, don't y'awl be calling me no grandpa.

MAMA ROSIE. What the hell else is they supposed to call you?

(*Earl swings around, and, seeing Mama Rosie, is disarmed into an unassuming manner.*)

EARL. (*Good-naturedly.*) Oh, Lordy! Me and you ain't gonna get into no fights before we even say hello, is we, Rosie?

ROSIE. (*Flat and to the point.*) What you driving?

RUTH ANN. A *Mr.* Eldorado, mama!

MAMA ROSIE. (*Not moving from her spot.*) You bring any money?

EARL. Now, Rosie, why can't you be nice?

MAMA ROSIE. How come I ain't being nice? I ain't cussed you out or nothing yet.

EARL. (*Throwing up his hands and giving an amused laugh.*) Girl, you ain't changed a bit.

NORMA. Daddy, gimme the car keys . . . me and Ruth Ann gonna take us a little spin.

EARL. Not in my car you ain't.

RUTH ANN. Aw, daddy . . . (*Rosie begins to mosey over to the window to look at the car.*)

NORMA. Aw, man, we ain't goin' hurt the damn thing. Gimme the keys.

EARL. Y'awl ain't doing no cruising and showing off in *my* car. Get out the way, Norma Faye! Don't be jooging your hands in my pocket!

NORMA. Well, gimme them keys, then.

MAMA ROSIE. Damn the keys. Get some money out-a there.

EARL. Wait a minute, now, Rosie . . .

NORMA. Yeah, that's cool . . . if you ain't gonna let us drive the car, give us some money.

EARL. (*Smoothing out his pants.*) I ain't studying y'awl.

MU'DEAR. Y'awl give your daddy a chance to sit down and rest . . . he *just* got in the door.

MAMA ROSIE. Yeah, and 'fore we know it, he'll be right back out that door and we won't see him again for *another* six years. Y'awl get that money.

EARL. Now, see there, Rosie, you fixing to start some trouble.

MAMA ROSIE. You the one started the trouble . . . waving all these diamonds and things in front-a us.

NORMA. Daddy, you ain't getting out-a this house 'til you get up off some-a that money.

RUTH ANN. Daddy, we do *need* some.

EARL. Y'awl got husbands, ain't you? I know you didn't let no man hit-and-run you, especially not Norma Faye! With her pistol-packing self.

NORMA. Aw, we don't wanna hear that.

MAMA ROSIE. Hold him, y'awl. I'll get it. (*Mama Rosie, Ruth Ann and Norma begin to converge on him. Earl gets belligerent trying to hold them off.*)

EARL. Wait a minute, y'awl! Don't be wrinkling up my suit! Get back! Don't be digging your hands in my pockets, that stretches the pants. Y'awl stretching my pants!

MAMA ROSIE. Well, how do *you* get the money out-a there?

EARL. I'll show you . . . just please get back! You know I'm gonna give y'awl the money.

MAMA ROSIE. (*Holding her hand out.*) Right now.

EARL. Good Lord! (*Everybody giggles . . . while Earl tries to smooth himself out from the ordeal. Norma and Ruth Ann keep giggling as Earl carefully slides his hands into his pocket and takes out his wallet.*) Y'awl the out-beggingest women ever I seen in my life . . . always got your hands out.

MAMA ROSIE. Well, how else is anybody gonna know we need something?

NORMA. Ooooo, daddy! Y'awl, I see something with a One and two O's!

EARL. Give 'em room to breathe, now. (*Earl begins licking his fingers before sliding off a bill and passing it out. Everyone except Mr. Herbert is given a bill. Elated "thank yous" are ad-libbed.*)

RUTH ANN. Ooooo, Lord-have-mercy! (*To little Earl.*) Let mama keep that for you 'til you get old enough, honey.

EARL. Boy, don't let no woman hold your money . . . they don't let go of it. Need a loan, Herbert? I can lay a few coins on you 'til you get straight.

MR. HERBERT. My credit is good anywhere in this town . . . I can get all the loans I need. (*Earl shrugs. Herbert falls into a sullen silence.*)

NORMA. Daddy, I got another baby at home.

RUTH ANN. And I got another one baking in the oven, daddy.

EARL. What! Y'awl crazy! I ain't giving y'awl no more-a my money.

MAMA ROSIE. (*Calling.*) Billie Jean! Come on in here and get some-a this money!

16

EARL. Now, wait a minute, Rosie, I ain't giving my money to every nigguh's kid in the neighborhood.

MAMA ROSIE. What the hell you mean, every nigguh's kid? You know who Billie Jean's daddy is . . . and I know damn well you ain't intending to come in this house and give everybody in here some-a that money and not give Billie Jean none.

EARL. Hell, I'm letting her wear my name, ain't that enough?

BILLIE JEAN. (*Appearing in the doorway.*) You can have it back anytime you want it, Earl.

EARL. Well, look-a there!

MAMA ROSIE. Billie Jean, I didn't call you in here to act smart. (*Norma and Ruth Ann begin swooning over their money. Mr. Herbert gives Billie a sympathetic look.*)

EARL. (*Appraising Billie Jean.*) Done growed up and got fine!

RUTH ANN. (*Kissing her money.*) U-lye-zes S. Grant, you is one dead white boy I don't mind kissing.

NORMA. It's been soooooo long.

RUTH ANN. Ain't we got a nice daddy, sis?

MU'DEAR. All right, y'awl . . . don't run it in the ground . . . you've seen money before.

EARL. When's the last time you seen your old no-good daddy, Billie Jean?

MAMA ROSIE. He better not bring his ass 'round here again . . . the chicken-shit bastard.

EARL. I heard he was going 'round telling people Billie Jean wasn't none-a his'n.

MAMA ROSIE. Up his mammy's ass with a flag-pole . . . hell, I ought-a know who her daddy is.

MU'DEAR. Rosie . . . don't.

MAMA ROSIE. Well, what he trying to say 'bout me, Deah? Hell, if he came around he'd see that Billie Jean is just like him . . . half-crazy and everything else. (*Norma and Ruth Ann can't seem to stop giggling.*)

MU'DEAR. Rosie, why don't you stop doing that . . . and y'awl stop that giggling 'cause it ain't funny what your mama is doing.

MAMA ROSIE. Deah, truth don't hurt nobody. (*Mu'Dear shakes her head in exasperation.*)

EARL. See . . . you had me and you wouldn't treat me right.

MAMA ROSIE. You wouldn't act right.

EARL. Wouldn't act right. Dig this girl, will ya', Deah! Didn't she have a roof over her head? And did these children want for anything?

MU'DEAR. They shore didn't want for nothing.

MAMA ROSIE. Well, I wanted for something.

EARL. Yeah, that was your trouble . . . you wasn't never satisfied. You wanna' style big, I know. But, see, if you'd just had a little patience . . .

MAMA ROSIE. Don't let it worry you. When I do get mine, you'll go into hiding and stay.

EARL. (*Laughing*.) All right, Rosie, keep your big dreams . . . come on get your money, Billie Jean.

BILLIE JEAN. Naw, that's all right, Earl . . . I don't want no money. (*Earl's mouth drops open*.)

MAMA ROSIE. Girl, are you crazy! You better not be turning down no money. If you don't want it, get it and give it to me.

EARL. Lord, I always wondered why that voice kept telling me to pack my things and git while the gitting was good . . . and now I know . . . *two* Rosies under the same roof! Herbert, you shore must have your balls together. (*Herbert is not complimented*.)

MAMA ROSIE. What the devil you talking about?

EARL. Billie Jean got ways just like you, Rosie.

MAMA ROSIE. You ain't never seen me turn down no money . . . I don't care if the *devil* is giving it. (*Everybody laughs*.)

MU'DEAR. I know I ain't never seen you do it . . . Lord knows I ain't.

EARL. You know what I'm talking about, Rosie . . . Billie Jean is just like you.

MAMA ROSIE. Shit, Billie Jean ain't nothing like me. That child up there is more like me than anybody I ever met. She *want* something out-a life. (*Rosie has pointed to the T.V. set, where sits the photo of Netta in her high school cap and gown*.)

EARL. (*Squinting at the photo*.) Who is that? I thought that was Billie Jean.

MAMA ROSIE. That's my other daughter. The one you don't know about.

EARL. When did you have that one, Rosie? You always springing some new kid on me. Is *she* wearing my name, too?

MAMA ROSIE. Naw-she-ain't. Hell, everybody ain't raring to wear your damn name. That child is too good to wear your name, anyway.

EARL. Now, wait a minute, Rosie.

NORMA. (*Sourly.*) How come she too good to wear daddy's name, mama?

RUTH ANN. (*Sourly.*) And if she all that goody-goody, how come her mother put her out-a her house? (*Earl is puzzled by and interested in understanding what the photo means, but he cannot keep his contemptuously appraising eyes from wandering to Billie Jean.*)

MAMA ROSIE. That's for me to know and for you to find out.

EARL. What's going on here? (*He reads aloud the inscription written on the photo . . . taken aback in surprise at the words.*) "To my dear Mama Rosie . . ." MAMA Rosie?

MAMA ROSIE. You can read, can't you?

EARL. ". . . God will surely bless you for helping so many of us when we needed help." (*He gives her a suspicious look.*)

MU'DEAR. Rosie didn't tell you, Earl, but she done took to keeping girls ever now and then. First it was just one-a Norma and Ruth Ann's friend that didn't have no place to stay. Now every stray alley cat in town done found 'em a good thing. (*Norma and Ruth Ann giggle.*)

MAMA ROSIE. Deah, I don't like that.

MU'DEAR. Rosie, all I said is they found 'em a good thing.

MAMA ROSIE. You know what you trying to make it sound like, Deah.

EARL. What it sounds like to me is that you and me is cooking in the same kitchen, Rosie, 'cause I keeps girls, myself.

MAMA ROSIE. Well, you can just get your mind out the gutter, 'cause these is nice girls. I might get a trifling one every now and then, but most of 'em makes me right proud of 'em.

EARL. You get any money for this, Rosie?

MAMA ROSIE. I don't want no money for it.

EARL. Let me get this straight. You mean, you just gives a girl a home what ain't got no home just out-a the goodness of your heart.

MAMA ROSIE. I loves those girls like my own daughters.

EARL. Oh. Norma Faye and Ruth Ann and Billie Jean wasn't enough for you, huh?

MAMA ROSIE. They don't 'preciate me like those girls do.

NORMA. Maybe if you would 'preciate *us* more, mama . . .

MAMA ROSIE. What is there to 'preciate? I don't see none-a

19

y'awl's graduation pictures up there. You and Ruth Ann couldn't keep your dresses down . . . and Billie Jean done quit school.

EARL. Oh, y'awl got caught, huh? (*Norma and Ruth Ann, embarrassed, regard their mother hostilely for exposing them.*)

MAMA ROSIE. Yeah, they got caught, and the way Billie Jean like to shake her tail, she's next. I don't put no faith in none of 'em no more. My girl Netta is gonna pull me through. When she get her diploma, she gonna come back here and teach.

NORMA. What's so big about a teacher, mama? You go in some white woman's kitchen and you liable to find one working there. What's the sense in wasting all that time in some fancy college just to work in a kitchen? (*Ruth Ann cackles nervously.*)

MAMA ROSIE. That ain't gonna happen to my Netta.

NORMA. Mama, how do you know?

MAMA ROSIE. 'Cause my girl is smart, that's why. That child won all kinds-a awards and scholarships. They can't mess with nobody that smart. Yeah, I know y'awl don't wanna hear this, but maybe if I rub it in hard enough, it'll help keep your gals from throwing their legs up for the first man that come along.

NORMA. In case you didn't know it, mama, my husband wasn't the first man.

RUTH ANN. Mine wasn't either.

MAMA ROSIE. (*Understanding exactly what they meant.*) Well, you see that, Earl? They stopped thinking about me a long time ago. You see what they had on they minds. Your off-springs. (*Earl, indifferent, has been stealing glances at Billie Jean.*)

EARL. They yours, too, baby.

NORMA. Look, mama, I happen to consider it a honor to be a mother to my children and a wife to my husband.

RUTH ANN. I'm proud-a what I'm doing, too.

MAMA ROSIE. If you so proud, how come you don't stay home with your husbands and children sometimes then, 'stead-a being over here damn near every day? You don't be coming to see me. Neither one of you don't like what you got into, but you can't get out. Any cow can lay down and get up with her stomach big. Ain't nothing to it. You just try to follow that child's example. That child gonna buy your mother a home some day.

NORMA. Oh, you believe that, huh, Mama?

MAMA ROSIE. Yes, I do.

NORMA. Mama, you talk like somebody with a wooden head.

That girl been up there at that college almost three years and ain't wrote you but two or three letters . . . she ain't thinking 'bout you.

MAMA ROSIE. That show how much you know about it, Norma Faye. I *told* her not to write too often, 'cause I wanted her to tend to her books.

EARL. Rosie, let me get this straight. You means to tell me that some girl you just took in off the street is gonna buy you a house . . . just like that?

MAMA ROSIE. Just like that.

MU'DEAR. You hope, Rosie.

MAMA ROSIE. I know. The spiritualist told me a child that wasn't mine would make me happy one day. (*Norma and Ruth Ann groan.*)

EARL. Rosie, you still spending money on them damn fortune tellers?

MU'DEAR. You can't tell her nothing, child . . . you just can't tell Rosie nothing.

EARL. Look, Rosie, you want a house? Billie Jean ain't got no kids yet . . . she can get you a house.

MAMA ROSIE. With what? All Billie Jean got her mind on is some old dancing mess.

EARL. Dancing?

NORMA. Yeah, daddy, she do that bal'let-dancing stuff . . . you know, where you kick your leg out and have your arms flapping like chicken wings . . . like them white folks do. (*Ruth Ann is trying to control herself.*)

EARL. That's what you wanna do, Billie Jean? (*Billie Jean does not answer.*)

NORMA. She practice it every day and haves a fit if anybody just knock on the door while she doing it.

EARL. Billie Jean, if you thinking 'bout making money off-a that stuff, you can just forget it, baby. Ain't no colored girls making nothing off-a that. The white chicks is even starving trying to do it. I knows what I'm talking 'bout, baby. That's a out-a-style scene. Can you do the funky chicken? (*Norma Faye and Ruth Ann giggle. Billie remains silent.*)

MAMA ROSIE. I told her that mess wasn't gonna buy her a pot to piss in or a window to throw it out of.

NORMA. It's paying her $3 a night at the Groovey Grill . . . that'll buy the pot.

EARL. At the Groovey in Two?! You doing *that* kind-a dancing at the Groovey in *Second Ward*, Billie Jean? (*Billie Jean does not answer.*)

NORMA. Man, what you talking 'bout . . . she the star dancer there.

EARL. Not at the Groovey Bar and Grill in *Two!* We *must* not be talking 'bout the same place.

NORMA. That's the place.

EARL. Damn! What is them nigguhs *drinking* out there?!! (*Ruth Ann cannot hold in her giggle. She and Norma laugh openly.*)

MAMA ROSIE. They just had her doing that old crazy stuff for a front. They was gonna have her switching to that strip-T later on. I know.

EARL. (*Relieved.*) Well, tell *me* something! But even at that . . . $3 a night. Damn, baby! You wanna use what your mama gave you *that* bad, come on back to De-troit with me. I'll show you how to get your P.H.D. in social work in a few weeks. (*Earl gives Billie Jean a little wink with innuendoes.*) I bet'cha that'll sell when cotton won't. (*Norma and Ruth Ann roar with laughter. Mr. Herbert, who has been leaning against a wall suffering through the ordeal with this boor, can stand it no longer. He straightens up, offended and angry.*)

MR. HERBERT. Look, Earl, don't do that. You know better than to talk like that with Deah sitting here. You respect her and I mean that. (*Earl looks embarrassed and charmingly innocent.*)

MAMA ROSIE. (*Coming to Earl's defense.*) Herbert, Deah ain't no virgin.

MR. HERBERT. That ain't the point . . . he ain't got no business talking like that in front-a none-a these women.

MAMA ROSIE. Well, hell. Every woman in here except Billie Jean is married . . . and according to what I just heard Billie Jean sneaking and doing, she *liable* to be in motherhood this very minute. And even if she ain't *yet*, at least Earl would take her somewhere where she wouldn't be around this town disgracing the family.

MR. HERBERT. Can't nobody disgrace nothing that's already a disgrace, Rosie.

22

MU'DEAR. Oh, y'awl, please don't start no mess . . . I ain't in no mood for it.

MAMA ROSIE. (*Glaring at Mr. Herbert.*) Herbert, what in the hell is you trying to say? You don't like this family, ain't nobody holding you in it.

MU'DEAR. That's enough, Rosie. 'Fore you say something you'll be sorry for.

MAMA ROSIE. If I say it, I ain't gonna be sorry. Herbert know I don't play that shit. (*Billie Jean, humiliated, leaves the doorway and disappears.*)

MU'DEAR. Just take it easy, Rosie. That's all.

MR. HERBERT. (*Leaving in a huff.*) I just wouldn't let no man talk like that in front-a no daugthers of mine.

MAMA ROSIE. Well, Herbert, you skin your cat and I'll skin mine. (*Norma and Ruth Ann try to muffle their giggles.*)

MU'DEAR. Rosie, y'awl are grown people, and . . .

MAMA ROSIE. (*Touchy and defensive.*) Deah, why you just call my name?

MU'DEAR. You know what you do, Rosie. You know exactly what you do. If a gorilla came through that door now, you'd try to provoke him.

MAMA ROSIE. Yeah, blame it all on me, Deah. I did it all.

MU'DEAR. Oh, my Father! Lord, show us the way!

EARL. (*Shrugging innocently.*) Hell. I was just trying to help. You said you wanted a house. And you said Billie Jean was wasting her time.

MAMA ROSIE. Ain't nobody said I needed your help to get me nothing, Earl. I got somebody who'll help me get all I want . . . don't you worry.

EARL. All right, Rosie. (*The grins are wiped off Norma's and Ruth Ann's faces. They exchange glances, then look coldly from their mother to the photo of Netta.*)

END OF ACT I

ACT II

Scene 1

*The living room. Earl is on his way out of the front door.
Norma is combing Sheryl's hair. Ruth Ann is standing in
front of the door to block Earl's exit.*

RUTH ANN. Daddy, stay a little while longer?

EARL. How come y'all didn't treat me this good when I was
married to your mama?

RUTH ANN. Aw, Daddy, we didn't even see much of you
then . . .

EARL. You don't see much of me now either, yet-and-still you
all over me. I know. I got some money now, yeah.

RUTH ANN. Aw, Daddy . . .

NORMA. Girl, don't be begging that man to stay. (*Norma then
calls out to Mama Rosie.*) . . . Mama, Daddy fixing to leave!

EARL. Now, see there, Norma Faye . . .

MAMA ROSIE. (*Off stage.*) Wait a minute, E. P. . . . gimme a
ride to work.

EARL. All right, now, y'awl ain't got no chauffeur to be ca'ing
y'awl all over town!

MAMA ROSIE. (*Off stage.*) I ain't asked you to drive me all
over town . . . I asked you to take me one place.

EARL. Yeah, well, don't make this no habit. That's why I hate
to bring my car here.

MAMA ROSIE. You wanna drive me to work or don't you?
(*Rosie is buttoning up her clothes and adjusting her earrings.*)

EARL. No-I-don't! Now, whatcha gonna say to that?

MAMA ROSIE. I say that's too bad . . . you gonna drive me
anyway. Go get my purse, Ann, so I can keep a eye on him.

EARL. (*Laughing.*) Now, what's gonna keep me from walking out
this door?

MAMA ROSIE. (*Good-naturedly.*) Not what, who. Me, that's
who. And what you gonna get me for Mother's Day?

24

EARL. You ain't none-a my mother, Rosie. (*Ruth Ann has re-appeared, and she and Norma laugh.*)

MAMA ROSIE. Be funny if you want to. Just make sure you make it over this way Mother's Day with a nice *big* present for me *and* Deah.

EARL. Rosie . . . your other husband liable to walk through that door while I'm here and start shooting or something . . . mess up my clothes.

NORMA. (*Laughing.*) Daddy, you and them clothes gotta go.

MAMA ROSIE. Now, look, I told you my divorce had come through and that bastard wasn't none-a my husband no more, so stop calling him that.

EARL. You ain't trying to start flirting with me again, is you, Rosie?

MAMA ROSIE. Hell, naw. Look, Earl, no kidding. Come over for Mother's Day. My other daughter might be coming home and I want you to meet her. I called her and asked her to try and come and she said she'll write and let me know if she can make it. So stop on by just in case she can make it.

EARL. Rosie, I don't wanna meet no daughter.

MAMA ROSIE. Well, you ought-a wanna meet her just so you can see what your own daughters *didn't* make out-a theyselfs. (*Norma's hand, in the middle of a stroke with the comb, freezes in the air. Ruth Ann shoots a glance at Norma.*)

EARL. Yeah, yeah, I'll think about it . . . hurry up, will ya, Rosie?

MAMA ROSIE. What you in such a damn hurry for? You ain't got no job to be rushing off to.

EARL. You know I don't like to stay in one place too long, Rosie.

MAMA ROSIE. Y'awl make sure you pay that insurance man today.

EARL. I might see y'awl later.

RUTH ANN. O.K., Daddy. (*Mama Rosie and Earl leave the house. Norma, a hard look on her face, is deep in thought.*)

NORMA. That bitch ain't staying in this house.

RUTH ANN. How you gonna stop her, Norma Faye? You don't even live here anymore.

NORMA. (*Loud and determined.*) I say she ain't staying in this house.

RUTH ANN. Well, I ain't deaf, Norma.

NORMA. (*After some thought.*) Sheryl, go outside and play with Earl. (*Sheryl runs outside. To Ruth Ann.*) Come on in Billie Jean's room with me . . . and be cool.

END OF SCENE I

ACT II

SCENE 2

> *Billie Jean's room. Billie Jean is slowly, methodically tearing up photos of the dancers which were hanging on her wall. A knock is heard at the door.*

NORMA. (*Off stage.*) Jean? Open the door, Jean. (*Billie scrambles to hide the torn pieces of the photos under her mattress, then goes to open the door. Norma and Ruth Ann enter.*) Jean, you got a place to stay for next year? (*Before Billie Jean can answer, Norma forces on.*)

BILLIE JEAN. What? . . . ?

NORMA. If you ain't married by next year you can come and live with me.

RUTH ANN. (*Right on cue.*) Jean, I would take you, but when the baby come, I don't know what Johnny would say with a extra person in the house . . .

NORMA. I don't care what my old man say . . . if I can't bring my family there when they out in the cold, then he don't want me there.

BILLIE JEAN. (*Puzzled.*) What y'awl talking about?

NORMA. What you mean, what we talking about?

BILLIE JEAN. I mean how come y'awl talking about a place for me to stay?

NORMA. You know you can't sleep on the couch. Mama don't let nobody sleep on her couch.

RUTH ANN. She ain't heard yet, Norma Faye . . . I told you Mama hadn't told her yet.

BILLIE JEAN. Ain't told me what? Is some other girl coming to live here?

26

NORMA. Naw, that's just it . . . ain't gonna be no more different girls. Mama say from now on it's just gonna be one, certain girl.

RUTH ANN. Mama don't never tell nobody nothing . . . she just go on do what she wanna do and everybody just fall in line.

NORMA. Jean, you mean to tell me Mama didn't tell you that when your friend get her diploma from that college next year, you gonna have to give up your room?

BILLIE JEAN. Give up my room? Naw, Mama didn't tell me that. And that girl ain't none-a my friend.

RUTH ANN. I don't see why they can't live in here together . . . but I guess she gots to have the whole room . . . all them clothes teachers have . . . changing two and three times a day . . . suits in the morning, casual slacks in the afternoon, cocktail rags at night . . . I guess she gots to have the whole room.

BILLIE JEAN. Y'awl kidding me?

NORMA. (*As if she didn't hear Billie Jean.*) The way Mama put it, though, Ruth Ann, she wanted Jean married and off-a her hands by next year 'cause she wasn't gonna see her Netta cramped all up in this room with another person.

BILLIE JEAN. Did Mama say that?

NORMA. That's right, Billie Jean, go ask her so she'll know we came and told you . . . (*Norma makes a motion as if to leave the room.*) . . . Shit, I'm sorry I told you.

BILLIE JEAN. Wait-a-minute, Norma, I'm not gonna say nothing. (*Norma stays.*)

RUTH ANN. What I think, Jean, is at least Mama could-a told you . . . yet-and-still I don't think it's fair to be put out-a your room for somebody that ain't even in the family.

BILLIE JEAN. (*Shuts off record.*) I ain't giving up my room to nobody.

NORMA. Ain't no sense in you talking big, Billie Jean. When Mama want something, everybody gotta jump and let her have her way. So you might as well make up your mind that, come next year, you'll be kissing this room good-by, baby.

RUTH ANN. If it was my room, somebody would be kicked good-by. I'd meet her at the door 'fore she got *through* the door.

NORMA. (*At door.*) I tried to tell you, Jean, three years ago when you was all friendly with her, you better watch that girl. I knew then mama had plans for her to come back here and get this

27

room. Naw, you wouldn't listen . . . Now you being kicked out-a your room for her.

BILLIE JEAN. Oh, you think I didn't watch her, huh? You think I been secret-buddy to her all these years, huh? Yeah, she come writing me letters when she first left, trying to sound all chummy and stuff, but I didn't even answer her. I'm tired-a hearing that girl's name . . . every time I turn around, mama throwing her up to me. "Why don't you follow Netta's example? My Netta gonna be teacher this and teacher that."

NORMA. Aw, mama is just pitiful. Working at that school is done messed her mind up. Have y'awl ever been with her when she tell people she work at the school?

RUTH ANN. "I'm on the staff at Carver High." She don't tell nobody she the maid. (*Giggles.*)

NORMA. Puttin' on all them airs and didn't go no further than the fourth grade!

BILLIE JEAN. Fourth grade?! Who, mama?!

NORMA. Mama, baby. That's right. I over-heard Mu'Dear say one day when they was having one-a their hot arguments that mama *had* to drop out-a school in the fourth grade. I didn't hear *why* mama *had* to drop out, 'cause mama shut *her* up with a little skeleton from the closet, too, but I got my guesses. And next time she throw that mess up in my face 'bout I had to get married, I'm gonna sound off on her.

BILLIE JEAN. (*Amazed.*) Fourth grade!

RUTH ANN. And them teachers don't do nothing but laugh at her.

NORMA. They laugh at *all* of us. We a big joke to 'em. Jean, you know the teachers we had. What did they do? Pass out them old raggedy-ass books the white schools didn't want no more, then mark us present if we was picking some white man's cotton . . . and pass us on. Hell, I don't need no diploma from Harvard to do that. So what is all this bragging mama doing 'bout some old ig'nant gal coming back to this hole to spoof the kids? And making Billie Jean give up her room for her . . .

BILLIE JEAN. She ain't getting my room! I'll burn it down 'fore I see her in it. (*Norma and Ruth Ann exchange looks.*)

NORMA. Well, if you feel that way 'bout her, Jean, how you gonna stand to stay here in the room with her when she come for Mother's Day?

BILLIE JEAN. She coming here for Mother's Day?

NORMA. Next week some time, so I heard.

RUTH ANN. I guess mama didn't tell you that, either, huh?

BILLIE JEAN. She didn't tell me nothing.

RUTH ANN. Damn!

NORMA. Maybe she was gonna tell her, Ruth Ann. Maybe she just waiting till she know definite 'fore she tell her.

RUTH ANN. Yeah, maybe so . . . all mama said was that she called and asked her to come. She won't know definite till the girl write and tell her what day.

BILLIE JEAN. Oh, a letter coming to tell mama, huh? Well, I know what to do with her letters when they come for mama. (*Billie lifts her mattress and produces a stack of letters all from Netta to Mama Rosie.*)

NORMA. (*Surprised.*) Well, I'll be damn!

RUTH ANN. (*Same.*) Mama ain't read them?

BILLIE JEAN. I didn't like the way she was talking in 'em . . . all 'preciative, you know.

RUTH ANN. (*Crosses to mattress.*) I told you Billie Jean got more sense than she make out sometime.

NORMA. Billie Jean, you our full-blooded sister now. And I promise you one thing . . . anybody . . . and I mean *anybody* . . . that come to take over your room is gonna be in for a big surprise.

RUTH ANN. And Jean, you *know* Norma Faye don't play.

BILLIE JEAN. (*In accord.*) I know. (*Norma and Ruth Ann slide their palms over each other. Then both girls extend their open palms to Billie Jean, who responds and grins broadly with relief and a new-found kinship.*)

END OF SCENE 2

ACT II

Scene 3

The living room. When the card table and two chairs are placed in the middle of the room and near the entrance to Billie Jean's room, there is hardly enough room to pass

by Norma and Ruth Ann, who are sitting at the table playing cards.
Billie Jean is looking out of the window.

BILLIE JEAN. Here she come, y'awl. (*At this point, Norma and Ruth Ann snap around in their chairs, so that their backs will be toward the front door. A mirror placed strategically on the table is there so that Norma and Ruth Ann can observe the action behind them without turning around.*)

RUTH ANN. Do your thing, sis.

NORMA. If she don't, I shore got my shit together.

BILLIE JEAN. Quiet, y'awl. (*Before the knock is heard at the door, Billie Jean flings the door open in an exaggerated welcome.*) Teach! Look who's here, y'awl, it's Teach! Welcome to the home of Billie-the-Kid . . . (*Netta, speechless, can manage only a weak: "Hi, Bill . . ."*) . . . gimme that bag, goddamit! Don't be totin' no heavy things around here. Educated folks don't supposed to work . . . don't you know that? (*Billie Jean snatches the suitcase from a surprised Netta.*) . . . git in this room and make yourself comfortable . . . (*Billie Jean whisks the suitcase away to her room, grumbling as she exits. Norma slides her chair up to let Billie Jean pass then slides back to fill up the space.*) . . . round here totin' bags with all these heavyweight champs in the house.

NETTA. Hey, where's Mama Rosie? (*Norma and Ruth Ann continue to play cards as if no one has entered. Netta looks around the room, perplexed.*)

NORMA. Wait-a damn minute, Ann. It's my pull.

RUTH ANN. Oh, I thought you pulled already.

NORMA. How the hell you thought I pulled when you just trumped my card?

RUTH ANN. Well, go 'head on, then, I be glad when you start winning, so you can stop being so grouchy. (*Netta moves toward the doorway leading to the front bedroom, looking for Mama Rosie.*)

NORMA. (*Back still turned.*) Up there at that fancy, white college they can't learn you how to speak to people when you see 'em, "Miss Teacher"?

NETTA. I was waiting to see your faces so I could . . .

NORMA. (*Facing Netta, but keeping the reins on her anger.*)

30

What the goddamn hell you have to *see* our faces for? You know we got 'em.

RUTH ANN. (*Touching her to calm her.*) Sis. (*Billie Jean re-enters carrying three wrapped gifts.*)

BILLIE JEAN. Look, y'awl. Santi-Claus is done come early.

NETTA. (*Making a move for them, then stopping.*) Those are for . . .

BILLIE JEAN. For us, Teach? Let's see now . . . (*Billie Jean counts beads.*) One, two, three. Gots to be for us.

NETTA. (*Trapped.*) Well, I . . . wanted them to be a surprise.

RUTH ANN. Ain't that nice. Which one's mine?

NETTA. Er . . . the small ones have perfume in them.

RUTH ANN. I'll take it. Give it here, Billie Jean. (*Billie Jean takes the gifts over to Ruth Ann and Norma. Norma leans over and sniffs under Ruth Ann's arm-pits. Billie Jean giggles.*)

NORMA. Yeah, hurry up and give it to her. (*Norma snatches one box from the stack Netta is holding and places it on the table before Ruth Ann.*)

RUTH ANN. Go to hell, ass-hole. (*Norma takes the big package.*)

NORMA. What's in this one?

NETTA. It's a book.

NORMA. I know you ain't brought me no damn book.

NETTA. The book is for Billie.

BILLIE JEAN. What I'm gonna' do with it?

RUTH ANN. You better take it, sis . . . when one-a them big words get whipped on you, you'll be glad you got it. (*Billie holds the book up by two fingers as if it were infected.*)

NORMA. I guess that last one's mine.

RUTH ANN. . . . You got perfume, too, Sis.

NORMA. Me and Ruth Ann we stink, huh?

NETTA. I wasn't thinking that at all.

BILLIE JEAN. (*Reading the title with exaggerated stupidity.*) The Dance En-cy . . . cloppe . . . p . . .

NETTA. I thought it would help you with your work.

BILLIE JEAN. (*Touchy.*) What work?

NETTA. Your dancing.

BILLIE JEAN. (*Tossing the book on the couch.*) I don't do that mess no more.

NETTA. (*Surprised.*) You don't dance anymore?

31

NORMA. You heard her. (*Billie Jean rushes into her clowning cue to keep from dwelling on the subject too long.*)

BILLIE JEAN. If you look in the direction of the t.v. set, Teach, you'll see that your eyes . . . dusty though they might be . . . still look out across this sometimes very crowded room. Many a gal have come and went, but we still see you shining through Million-Dollar-Movie, Superman, and even the cartoons. You never go off the air.

NETTA. Did Mama Rosie go to work today?

NORMA. How the hell else is she gonna' feed all these stray boarders that's always popping in on her?

BILLIE JEAN. Yuck, yuck . . . sho'nuff.

NETTA. She called and asked me to come . . . and I wrote back and told her I'd be . . .

RUTH ANN. Yeah, well, mail don't go as fast here as it do in them big college towns, see.

NETTA. But, I mailed it over a week ago. And since Mama Rosie wanted to be off when I got here, she told me to write the exact day and hour . . . and I did. (*Norma and Ruth Ann do not react. Billie, after failing to catch her sisters' eyes for the cue, ventures forth.*)

BILLIE JEAN. Er-er, er-er, is you shore you writ in the very hour?

NETTA. I'm very sure, Billie . . .

BILLIE JEAN. (*Digging into her pocket and producing the letter.*) Let me see, now . . . "Dear Mama Rosie . . . so and so and so. Next Sad'day, the twenty-five, at . . . " Well, h'it damn shore is in here . . . Shore'nuff h'it is. (*Billie Jean, her head tilted to one side like an idiot, bares a row of grinning teeth to Netta.*)

NETTA. You mean Mama Rosie doesn't get her mail?

BILLIE JEAN. Aw, naw, naw . . . see, I is in charge of inter-house mail . . . and, er-er, beingst that I has been so busy lately, I just ain't had a chance to route this one yet.

NORMA. I hope something is coming through real clear to you, "Miss Teacher."

NETTA. It's clear to me why Billie Jean never answered about that talent search and that national tour I wrote her about. (*Norma and Ruth Ann feign innocence but look guilty.*)

BILLIE JEAN. What talent search? What national tour?

NETTA. Telling you would be like giving you your letter. And that seems to be against the rules around here.

RUTH ANN. She's trying to say we stole Billie Jean's letter, Sis.

NORMA. Yeah. And I don't like it worth a damn.

BILLIE JEAN. Then how come I didn't get it?

NORMA. She don't have to be done sent it just 'cause she say she did.

RUTH ANN. Yeah, her mouth ain't no prayer book, Jean.

NETTA. It had to do with this new dance company they're forming, Billie, for a national tour—and since you have to be enrolled as a student, I sent you an application for enrollment, too.

BILLIE JEAN. Enrollment in college?

RUTH ANN. (Cackling.) Billie Jean didn't even finish high school . . . talking 'bout college.

NETTA. (Surprised.) You didn't finish Billie?

BILLIE JEAN. (Embarrassed.) I could-a if I'd wanted to.

NORMA. She-it.

RUTH ANN. I ain't talking 'bout the could-a, I'm talking 'bout the did.

NETTA. You mean you got right to the end . . .

BILLIE JEAN. I could-a finished . . . this teacher made me mad, that's all . . . come talking about any nigger off the street can sing and dance.

RUTH ANN. They can. Miss Hallie's kid down the street ain't but eight years old, and she can do the same old country-ass kicking you do.

BILLIE JEAN. Well, whatever you call it, Ruth Ann, it was me that taught her those movements.

RUTH ANN. That's what I'm trying to get across to you, fool, if a eight-year-old child can do that stuff, you look like a fool bursting up to a big old college with something people can get in kindergarten . . . national tour . . . (Norma bowls with laughter, dampening Billie's spirits.) . . . I don't believe that shit myself.

NETTA. Every word I said is true, Billie. And I know you can make the company. Just get this high school thing over with . . . this summer maybe.

BILLIE JEAN. But will they take me at that big college?!

NORMA. Oh, girl, please! Ain't no sense in nobody as old as you being as dumb as you is, Billie Jean!

RUTH ANN. Ain't she pitiful??

NORMA. Mama set right here and read them newspapers 'bout

33

how them crackers up there was spittin' and throwin' piss all out the window on black folks.

NETTA. That was three years ago, Billie. Even white folks get tired-a acting a fool sometimes.

NORMA. She-it. I ain't got no fancy diplooma from Harvard or none-a them other high fallutin' places, but I ain't dumb enough to let nobody drag me to where no crackers is spittin' and shittin' on people.

RUTH ANN. And hell, Billie Jean, you can't even talk right . . . all that old country-ass talk you do.

BILLIE JEAN. I don't dance with my mouth. (*Norma begins looking under chairs and all around. Ruth Ann follows suit.*)

NORMA. Say, where did Billie Jean go, Ruth Ann?

RUTH ANN. Search me.

BILLIE JEAN. What's the matter with y'awl, drunk? Here I am.

NORMA. Oh. For a minute there I thought you had done cut out on us.

NETTA. You know you can drop that ole dumb act anytime. Think of how proud Mama Rosie will be when . . .

NORMA. (*Furious.*) Look, girl, what is all this shit 'bout you callin my mother "mama"? She ain't none-a your goddamn mama! Your mammy live ten blocks from here. You wanna' call somebody mama, walk ten fucking blocks.

NETTA. (*Trying to control herself.*) Norma, I've never called your mother a "mammy" and I don't think you should call my mother that.

NORMA. If you care so damn much for her, why in hell don't you go stay with her?

RUTH ANN. You ain't gonna take over Billie Jean's room.

NETTA. Take over Billie's room? Is that what you think, Billie?

BILLIE JEAN. (*Torn between the forces.*) Well, I . . .

RUTH ANN. That's what we all think.

NETTA. I'm going straight into law school when I finish next year, Billie. I'll be there awhile . . . and you'll be in the same place finishing up your education, won't you, Billie?

BILLIE JEAN. Well . . . I . . .

NORMA. (*Furious.*) Why in the hell don't you leave my sister alone?

RUTH ANN. Say, how is them little old white boys, Miss College? Beingst that you has had a chance to get at 'em.

34

NETTA. (*Flatly.*) I wouldn't know, Ruth Ann.

RUTH ANN. I know you ain't saying you been up there all this time and ain't tried none of 'em yet.

NETTA. That's exactly what I'm saying.

RUTH ANN. (*Exchanges looks with Norma.*) Damn!

NORMA. Have you tried *any* man yet?

NETTA. Beingst that that ain't what I went up there for, I don't consider it a lost cause. (*Norma and Ruth Ann exchange looks.*)

RUTH ANN. Who you saving it for, Jesus?

NORMA. (*Seriously.*) Girl, if you don't get your head out-a them books and get you a man you gonna go crazy.

RUTH ANN. Or end up funny, one.

NORMA. That's a disgrace . . . a twenty-one-year-old grown woman still walking 'round here guarding that stuff like it's the First National Bank.

RUTH ANN. (*None of this is funny to her.*) I always said too much-a that book stuff'll kill off a girl's femin' stuff.

NORMA. And trying to drag Billie Jean into that shit. (*Norma holds up a warning finger.*) Look, let me tell you something, Billie Jean . . . she done put all that mess on your brain about this college stuff and I can see you falling for it. Well, you go 'head. But if you disgrace this family by ending up funny . . . You better change your last name and you better not show your face around here again.

BILLIE JEAN. (*Too intimidated to fight.*) Aw, I'm not going to no college, Norma. I was just listening. I'm staying right here with you and Ruth Ann.

RUTH ANN. Look, Billie Jean, don't get us wrong. Me and Norma, we'd be proud to see you go off to college and buy you some nice rags, see? Them things she wearing, you'd look good in stuff like that. (*While Ruth Ann is talking, Norma goes over to Netta and begins feeling the texture of the material the blouse is made of. Netta gives her a cold look and says nothing.*) But what me and Norma is saying, Billie Jean . . . we want you to come back with your femin' stuff still together, see?

NORMA. Yeah, these some nice dry goods, all right.

RUTH ANN. While you over there, Norm, raise her dress up and see if she got one-a them things. I always wanted to see what one-a these freaks look like. (*Netta stiffens and glares at Norma who is*

*turning the thought over in her mind. Billie Jean, eyes wide, looks
on uneasily.)*

NORMA. I believe you done hit on something, Ruth Ann.

RUTH ANN. Shore I have. Remember how she used to jump and
cover herself up everytime one of us was 'bout to see her naked?

NORMA. Ain't this a bitch! All this time we wasn't even safe in
this house. *(Norma reaches for Netta's skirt. She stops, her hand
poised in the air, when Netta speaks.)*

NETTA. *(Flatly and precisely, trying to hold onto her anger.)*
Don't-put-your-hands-on-my-clothes, Norma.

RUTH ANN. Watch her, sis. If she is a man, she probably fight
like one. *(Norma straightens up and backs off a little, her fists
doubled up and ready for the fight. Netta turns and begins walking
toward the bedroom.)* Where you going?

NETTA. To get my things . . . so everybody can be safe in this
house.

BILLIE JEAN. But where're you gonna' stay?

NORMA. What the hell do you care where she's gonna' stay? Let
her take her ass to her insane mammy's house. *(A long moment of
a heavy silence in which a stung Netta smoulders with anger.)*

BILLIE JEAN. Norma . . .

NORMA. Didn't think we knew 'bout the lunatic-y bitch, did you?
Even the 'sane-a-sylum won't take her ass.

BILLIE JEAN. Norma, don't. *(Netta advances toward Norma.)*

RUTH ANN. Beware-bad-dog, sis . . . she gettin' hancty. *(Norma
whips a long knife from her bosom . . . clicks it. Netta stops
short.)*

NORMA. Come on, bitch . . . come on. Fuck with the bear.
*(Billie Jean instinctively reaches to hold Norma back . . . Norma
tears savagely away.)*

BILLIE JEAN. Aw, naw, Norma, she's fixing to leave . . .

NORMA. Fool, if you don't get out the way I'll make another
path up your ass! You know better'n to be tryin' to hold me when
somebody walkin' up on me! *(Ruth Ann, genuinely frightened,
tries to calm Norma down.)*

RUTH ANN. Sis . . . Sis . . . everything's cool, baby. Everything's cool, Norma, baby. You're a winner, baby . . . you're a
winner . . .

NORMA. What'cha waitin' for, tramp? Get your ass in gear, 'fore the butcher start slicing some balogna. (*Netta leaves . . . disappearing into the bedroom.*)

RUTH ANN. Damn, Sis! I ain't never seen you that mad.

NORMA. I wanted to tee-off on her so bad I could just taste it.

RUTH ANN. I know you did. (*Billie Jean picks the book up from the couch and heads toward the room where Netta disappeared.*)

NORMA. Where you going?

BILLIE JEAN. To give this back to her. She might wanna' pack it in the suitcase . . . and I wanna' make sure she don't take none-a my things. (*Ruth Ann knocks the boxed gifts to the floor.*)

RUTH ANN. Take those with you. Right, Norma?

NORMA. Right. But you ought-a keep the book, Billie Jean . . . it'll make good kindling for somebody's fire. (*Ruth Ann giggles nervously. Billie Jean picks up the boxes and heads uneasily toward the bedroom.*)

END OF SCENE 3

ACT II

SCENE 4

Billie Jean's room. Netta is crying.

BILLIE JEAN. Netta, I'm sorry. I didn't mean to do that.

NETTA. What did my mother ever do to her?

BILLIE JEAN. I didn't know they were gonna' go that far.

NETTA. Billie, get away from this place. Leave now.

BILLIE JEAN. I can't.

NETTA. Yes, you can. They don't have anything to give you. And can't you see they'll always be the same? If you stay here, you'll get just like them.

BILLIE JEAN. Netta, I'm not strong like you. (*Billie Jean cries and Netta comforts her.*)

NETTA. Yes, you are, Billie. Don't let them make you think you're weak and nothing. Get away from here.

BILLIE JEAN. I just wanna know one thing. Did my mother ever . . . well, did she ever tell you anything?

NETTA. Tell me what?

BILLIE JEAN. Well, you know . . . like, did she ever . . . just put her arms around you and . . . tell you she . . . you know what I'm talking about. You know I can't say that word. Just tell me if she ever said it to you. Tell me.
NETTA. She never said it.
BILLIE JEAN. (*Relieved and surprised.*) She never said it?
NETTA. That's not her way. But you know it's there. It's just something you believe is there.
BILLIE JEAN. Really?
NETTA. I know she loves you . . . but she just . . . (*Norma enters.*)
NORMA. How long it take you to put two damn boxes in a suitcase?
NETTA. It depends on how big the suitcase is and how small the boxes.
NORMA. You tryin' to play on my intelligence?
NETTA. I'm just trying to get out-a this house, Norma.
NORMA. Hell, you done had more than enough time to do that.
BILLIE JEAN. It just didn't seem to close right, Norma. I was watching.
NORMA. Ain't nobody asked you nothing. (*Netta locks the suitcase . . . heads for the door.*)
NETTA. Good-bye, Billie. (*Billie Jean does not answer. She turns away sullenly. Netta exits.*)
BILLIE JEAN. I don't know why she so friendly.
NORMA. Just don't try to make no fool out-a me, Billie Jean.

END OF SCENE 4

ACT II

SCENE 5

The living room. Mama Rosie, Norma and Ruth Ann are present. It is obvious that Norma and Ruth Ann have been talking to Mama Rosie, for she is sitting, listening thoughtfully to what is being said.

NORMA. (*Summing up.*) . . . and that's the way I feel about it, mama. I'm really scared she gonna get killed in one-a them places . . .

RUTH ANN. Me, too, mama. And you work hard everyday . . . you can't look after everything. You have did the best you could do for us.

NORMA. You sure have, mama. And we just got to take time out from our own lives and try to save Billie Jean. (*We hear the sound of Billie Jean bounding up on the porch. She enters the living room from the front door. Dressed in her dungarees and holding in her hand a small paper bag, she is out of breath. Right away she senses that something is up.*)

MAMA ROSIE. Billie Jean, go in your room, look through them clothes you got and find you something decent to wear for tonight.

BILLIE JEAN. Where am I going tonight, mama?

MAMA ROSIE. You gonna be right here, Billie Jean.

BILLIE JEAN. Well, are we having company or something?

MAMA ROSIE. . . . A nice boy is coming to see you.

BILLIE JEAN. Mama, what boy is this?

MAMA ROSIE. He's a nice boy, Billie Jean. (*Billie Jean senses what is happening.*)

BILLIE JEAN. I don't wanna meet no boy, mama.

MAMA ROSIE. Why, Billie Jean? The boy got a good job. I'll meet him myself and if he ain't what they say he is, you don't have to marry him.

BILLIE JEAN. Mama, when I'm ready to have boys, I'll pick my own boy.

MAMA ROSIE. What you mean when you *ready* to have boys? According to what I been hearing about *you*, Billie Jean . . .

BILLIE JEAN. Hearing what about me, mama?

MAMA ROSIE. You know what I been hearing.

BILLIE JEAN. Who's been telling you this?

MAMA ROSIE. Never mind who's been telling me . . . you're almost eighteen years old and ain't got no job or no husband or nothing. You ain't gonna hang out in these old honky-tonks until some old drunk nigguh kill you. I rather kill you, myself.

BILLIE JEAN. I'm not gonna hang out in no honky-tonk, mama.

MAMA ROSIE. Then, what is you gonna do, Billie Jean? (*Billie does not answer.*) You don't know, do you?

BILLIE JEAN. I do know, mama.

MAMA ROSIE. Well, what you gonna do?

BILLIE JEAN. I'm going up to where Netta is to finish high school and go to college.

MAMA ROSIE. Are you crazy, girl? You ain't going up there and bother *that* child.

NORMA. Mama . . . if she wanted to finish high school, how come she can't do it here? She just wanna get to another town and . . . hang around in these old joints . . . with men.

BILLIE JEAN. That's not what I wanna do!

MAMA ROSIE. Billie Jean, you sound like you losing your mind.

NORMA. She need to be in a reform school, mama, 'cause she gonna get hurt. (*Rising.*) I'll call the truant officer, mama. (*Billie Jean then breaks for the front door.*)

MAMA ROSIE. Where're you going? You come back here!

RUTH ANN. Hold her, Norma. (*Norma and Ruth Ann make a quick grab for Billie Jean. She hits one of her sisters with the paper bag.*)

NORMA. I told you, mama. This girl is just beside herself! (*Billie Jean struggles to free herself from them.*)

BILLIE JEAN. Y'awl leave me alone! Leave me alone.

MAMA ROSIE. Don't you kick me, girl! (*Mr. Herbert enters from the bedroom.*)

MR. HERBERT. What's the trouble here?

NORMA. It ain't nothing we can't handle, Mr. Herbert.

BILLIE JEAN. Mr. Herbert, make 'em turn me loose.

MR. HERBERT. What did she do? Y'awl leave that child alone 'fore I call Deah.

MAMA ROSIE. Ain't nobody called you in here, Herbert . . .

BILLIE JEAN. Call Mu'Deah for me, Mr. Herbert.

MAMA ROSIE. You better not.

MR. HERBERT. Ain't nobody scared-a you, Rosie. You knows I ain't. (*He calls out.*) Deah! You better come in here and see 'bout this mess!

MAMA ROSIE. You get your ass out-a my house. I mean I better not see you here in the morning.

BILLIE JEAN. I ain't did nothing . . . I ain't did nothing . . . (*Mu'Dear rushes into the room.*)

MU'DEAR. What's all the screaming in here? What's going on, Rosie?

MAMA ROSIE. Call the truant officer, Dear.

BILLIE JEAN. I didn't do nothing, Mu'Dear . . . please . . . don't let 'em do this to me.

MU'DEAR. Don't be twisting on that child like that!

MAMA ROSIE. Deah, you just go call the truant officer like I told you.

BILLIE JEAN. Mu'Dear . . . I swear to God I didn't do nothing . . .

NORMA. Mama, just hold this leg. I'll go call 'em.

MU'DEAR. Ain't nobody calling nobody till I find out what this is all about.

MAMA ROSIE. Deah, you don't run this house.

MU'DEAR. I didn't say I ran this house, Rosie . . . but I don't like what I see here.

MAMA ROSIE. You don't have to like it.

BILLIE JEAN. Mu'Deah . . . they hurting me all over.

MU'DEAR. Get up off her, Rosie . . . all of you, get up off her.

MAMA ROSIE. Deah, Billie Jean is *my* child!

BILLIE JEAN. I'm going to college, Mu'Dear . . . that's all I said to them.

NORMA. Yeah, that's what you *said* . . . but we know what you gonna *do*.

MU'DEAR. Rosie, sho'nuff Billie Jean is your child, but I got a feeling you're wrong.

MAMA ROSIE. Yeah, Deah, you ain't never thought I had sense enough to be right about nothing.

MU'DEAR. Oh, but, my dear daughter, you ain't never wanted to be wrong about nothing . . .

MAMA ROSIE. You're a lie, Deah! (*Mu'Dear, offended, straightens her body . . . her chin set . . . her fists clenched at her sides.*)

MU'DEAR. Listen to me, Rosie . . . listen carefully to what I'm saying. You've never in your life called me a lie. And, believe what I'm saying, child . . . God's gonna whip you for that. When you're laying on your death-bed, God's gonna whip you. Cause I'm your mother, Rosie . . . I'm your mother.

MAMA ROSIE. (*Rising fearfully, with bridled indignation.*) Deah, you ain't got no right to mark me like that. You just don't understand . . .

MU'DEAR. I understand one thing, my daughter . . . you better wake up. You don't know nothing about nobody in this house, 'cause you too busy trying to save strangers. If anybody just touch

one-a them gals you bring in here off the street, you bring down
the wrath of God . . . but with your own family, Rosie . . .

MAMA ROSIE. Deah, I loves all-a y'awl and you know it. I have
did all I could for Billie Jean.

MU'DEAR. Then let her have her life, Rosie. Don't try to tear
down the house just 'cause it ain't being built the way you want it.

MAMA ROSIE. (*Flustered.*) You ain't being fair, Deah. You trying to make it sound like I'm trying to hurt Billie Jean, and you're
wrong and you know it . . .

MU'DEAR. God didn't make you perfect in your judgment, either,
Rosie . . . you could be wrong about Billie Jean. God knows I
ain't crazy about her wanting to be no dancer, either, but that's
her life, Rosie. If she don't make nothing out-a it, it'll be her
nothing.

NORMA. Mu'Dear, you want us to just let her ruin her life?

MU'DEAR. She can't do no worse with her'n than you done done
with your'n. None of you! (*There is a stunned silence.*) Now, take
your hands off-a that child and be quick about it. (*Norma and
Ruth Ann let go of Billie Jean, who breaks into uncontrollable sobs.*)

END OF SCENE 5

ACT II

SCENE 6

The living room.
*Mama Rosie is present. She is sitting in a chair, her arms
folded sullenly across her chest.*
*Billie Jean, all dressed and packed, enters the living room
and hesitates uncomfortably when she sees her mother.*
Mama Rosie sits still and tries not to look at Billie Jean.
A taxi horn sounds outside. Billie approaches her mother.

BILLIE JEAN. (*Searching for words.*) Mama, I'm fixing to go
now. (*Mama Rosie does not answer.*) When I get there, I'll write
you and let you know I got there all right. (*Rosie still does not
answer.*) I think it takes about eight hours . . . or something like
that. (*Billie Jean searches for more words. The horn sounds again.*)

42

Thanksgiving is the next big holiday, mama, and . . . if I have the money, I'll come home. (*Mu'Dear enters from her bedroom.*)

MU'DEAR. That's your cab, honey. You take care-a yourself, now, you hear? (*They embrace.*)

BILLIE JEAN. Yes, ma'am. I'll be writing to you, Mu'Dear. (*Rosie glances at them, then looks away.*)

MU'DEAR. And don't you stay 'way no six years.

BILLIE JEAN. I won't, Mu'Dear.

MU'DEAR. Hurry up, now. You know they charge for waiting. (*Billie Jean moves toward the door . . . stops and turns when Rosie calls.*)

MAMA ROSIE. Billie Jean.

BILLIE JEAN. Ma'am?

MAMA ROSIE. I ain't never in my life apologized to nobody for nothing. It just ain't in me. (*Long pause.*)

BILLIE JEAN. Yes, ma'am.

MAMA ROSIE. Just . . . drop me a card or something ever now and then . . . let me know how your dancing is coming. (*Billie Jean goes back and hugs her. She rushes out of the house. She cannot hold in her tears. Mu'Dear stands looking sympathetically at Mama Rosie.*) She know I didn't mean to hurt her, Deah. It just looked like *all* my children was gon end up like me . . . like me. (*Rosie cannot control the trembling of her lips but she makes an iron effort until tears betray her.*)

THE END

43.

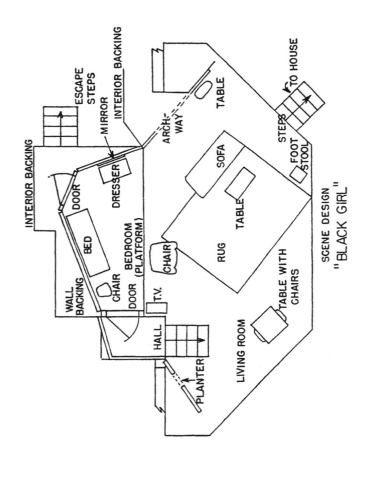

SCENE DESIGN "BLACK GIRL"

INTERIOR BACKING

ESCAPE STEPS

INTERIOR BACKING

MIRROR

INTERIOR BACKING

TO HOUSE

TABLE

ARCH-WAY

STEPS

FOOT STOOL

DRESSER

SOFA

DOOR

TABLE

RUG

BED

CHAIR

WALL BACKING

CHAIR

BEDROOM (PLATFORM)

DOOR

T.V.

HALL

TABLE WITH CHAIRS

PLANTER

LIVING ROOM

LIVING ROOM

SET PROPS:
Couch (with pillows)
Card table
Two armless chairs (at card table)
Armchair (with pillows and doilies)
Coffee table
Television
Table (small with potted plant)

SMALL PROPS:
Ironing board, iron with extension cord
White uniform on ironing board
Photograph of Netta (on television)

On Card Table:
Deck of cards
Ashtray
Box of crayons
Book of matches
Coloring book
Magazines and comic books

On Coffee Table:
Coloring book
Book of matches
Box of crayons
Magazines and comic books
Book
Ashtray
Mirror, to stand on card table

BEDROOM

SET PROPS:
Bunk beds
Small bed
Three drawer chest
Mirror (over chest)
Armless chair

SMALL PROPS:
  Record player (on chest)
  Record rack with records (on chest)
  Broken record in jacket (in record rack)
  Package of letters (under mattress)
  Books and magazines (2 on bed and 2 on chair)
  Pair of slippers on floor next to chest
  Pictures of ballet dancers on walls
  Coat hanging on hook by mirror
  Clothes on hooks
  Water color reproduction of Jesus in the Garden of Gethsemane
    (over TV)

HAND PROPS

BILLIE JEAN:
  Suitcase
  Bag of groceries
  Letter (opened)

EARL:
  Money, in wallet

MU'DEAR:
  Apron

NETTA:
  Suitcase
  Shopping bag with gift wrapped book and 2 perfume boxes

NORMA:
  Switch blade
  Comb

MAMA ROSIE:
  House coat
  Shoes
  Head cloth

RUTH ANN (for Mama Rosie):
  Purse and sweater

MR. HERBERT:
  Towel
  Toothbrush
  Cigar

COSTUME PLOT

ACT ONE

MAMA ROSIE:

Scene One—LIVING ROOM
Flowered house dress, black house slippers

Scene Two—BILLIE JEAN'S ROOM
Flowered house dress, black house slippers

Scene Two—LIVING ROOM
White uniform, brown sandals

BILLIE JEAN:

Scene One—LIVING ROOM
Yellow sweat shirt, white tennis shoes, blue jeans

Scene Two—BILLIE JEAN'S ROOM
Yellow sweat shirt, white tennis shoes, blue jeans

Scene Two—LIVING ROOM
Yellow sweat shirt, white tennis shoes, blue jeans

NORMA FAYE:

Scene One—LIVING ROOM
Short brown A-line skirt, long sleeved orange blouse, brown sandals

Scene Two—BILLIE JEAN'S ROOM
Short brown A-line skirt, long sleeved orange blouse, brown sandals

Scene Two—LIVING ROOM
Short brown A-line skirt, long sleeved orange blouse, brown sandals

RUTH ANN:

Scene One—LIVING ROOM
Green maternity top, blue jeans, black sandals

Scene Two—BILLIE JEAN'S ROOM
Green maternity top, blue jeans, black sandals

Scene Two—LIVING ROOM
Green maternity top, blue jeans, black sandals

MU'DEAR:

Scene Two—BILLIE JEAN'S ROOM
Light blue dress, white sandals

Scene Two—LIVING ROOM
Red print dress, white sandals

47

SHERYL ANN:

Scene One—LIVING ROOM
Blue plaid dress, blue tennis shoes

Scene Two—BILLIE JEAN'S ROOM
Blue plaid dress, blue tennis shoes

Scene Two—LIVING ROOM
Blue plaid dress, blue tennis shoes

LITTLE EARL:

Scene One—LIVING ROOM
Blue jeans, white tennis shoes, colored tee shirt

Scene Two—BILLIE JEAN'S ROOM
Blue jeans, white tennis shoes, colored tee shirt

Scene Two—LIVING ROOM
Blue jeans, white tennis shoes, colored tee shirt

MR. HERBERT:

Scene Two—BILLIE JEAN'S ROOM
White tee shirt, dark suit pants, suspenders

Scene Two—LIVING ROOM
Red striped shirt, dark suit pants, suspenders

EARL:

Scene Two—LIVING ROOM
Purple suit, red bow tie, purple ruffled shirt, orange socks, black
suede shoes

ACT Two

MAMA ROSIE:

Scene One—LIVING ROOM
White uniform, brown sandals, blue sweater, brown hand bag

Scene Four—LIVING ROOM
Green print short sleeved dress, black house slippers

Scene Five—LIVING ROOM
Green print short sleeved dress, black house slippers

BILLIE JEAN:

Scene Two—BILLIE JEAN'S ROOM
Yellow sweat shirt, white tennis shoes, blue jeans

Scene Three—LIVING ROOM AND BILLIE JEAN'S ROOM
Red sweater blouse, white tennis shoes, blue jeans

Scene Four—LIVING ROOM
Red sweater blouse, white tennis shoes, blue jeans

Scene Five—LIVING ROOM
Red sweater blouse, white tennis shoes, blue jeans, brown rain coat

NORMA FAYE:

Scene One—LIVING ROOM
Short brown A-line skirt, long sleeved orange blouse, brown sandals

Scene Two—BILLIE JEAN'S ROOM
Short brown A-line skirt, long sleeved orange blouse, brown sandals

Scene Three—LIVING ROOM AND BILLIE JEAN'S ROOM
Short brown A-line skirt, short sleeved light blue pull-over, brown sandals

Scene Four—LIVING ROOM
Short brown A-line skirt, short sleeved light blue pull-over, brown sandals

RUTH ANN:

Scene One—LIVING ROOM
Green maternity top, blue jeans, black sandals

Scene Two—BILLIE JEAN'S ROOM
Green maternity top, blue jeans, black sandals

Scene Three—LIVING ROOM AND BILLIE JEAN'S ROOM
Pink maternity top, blue jeans, black sandals

Scene Four—LIVING ROOM
Pink maternity top, blue jeans, black sandals

MU'DEAR:

Scene Four—LIVING ROOM
Light blue dress, apron, white sandals

Scene Five—LIVING ROOM
Light blue dress, white sandals

SHERYL ANN:

Scene One—LIVING ROOM
Blue plaid dress, blue tennis shoes

LITTLE EARL:

Scene One—LIVING ROOM
Blue jeans, white tennis shoes, colored tee shirt

MR. HERBERT:

Scene One—LIVING ROOM
Red striped shirt, dark suit pants, suspenders

Scene Four—LIVING ROOM
Red striped shirt, dark suit pants, suspenders

EARL:

Scene One—LIVING ROOM
Purple suit, red bow tie, purple ruffled shirt, orange socks, black suede shoes

NETTA:

Scene Three—LIVING ROOM AND BILLIE JEAN'S ROOM
Peach two-piece suit, peach pumps, white gloves

NEW PLAYS

★ **CLYBOURNE PARK by Bruce Norris.** WINNER OF THE 2011 PULITZER PRIZE AND 2012 TONY AWARD. Act One takes place in 1959 as community leaders try to stop the sale of a home to a black family. Act Two is set in the same house in the present day as the now predominantly African-American neighborhood battles to hold its ground. "Vital, sharp-witted and ferociously smart." –*NY Times.* "A theatrical treasure…Indisputably, uproariously funny." –*Entertainment Weekly.* [4M, 3W] ISBN: 978-0-8222-2697-0

★ **WATER BY THE SPOONFUL by Quiara Alegría Hudes.** WINNER OF THE 2012 PULITZER PRIZE. A Puerto Rican veteran is surrounded by the North Philadelphia demons he tried to escape in the service. "This is a very funny, warm, and yes uplifting play." –*Hartford Courant.* "The play is a combination poem, prayer and app on how to cope in an age of uncertainty, speed and chaos." –*Variety.* [4M, 3W] ISBN: 978-0-8222-2716-8

★ **RED by John Logan.** WINNER OF THE 2010 TONY AWARD. Mark Rothko has just landed the biggest commission in the history of modern art. But when his young assistant, Ken, gains the confidence to challenge him, Rothko faces the agonizing possibility that his crowning achievement could also become his undoing. "Intense and exciting." –*NY Times.* "Smart, eloquent entertainment." –*New Yorker.* [2M] ISBN: 978-0-8222-2483-9

★ **VENUS IN FUR by David Ives.** Thomas, a beleaguered playwright/director, is desperate to find an actress to play Vanda, the female lead in his adaptation of the classic sadomasochistic tale *Venus in Fur.* "Ninety minutes of good, kinky fun." –*NY Times.* "A fast-paced journey into one man's entrapment by a clever, vengeful female." –*Associated Press.* [1M, 1W] ISBN: 978-0-8222-2603-1

★ **OTHER DESERT CITIES by Jon Robin Baitz.** Brooke returns home to Palm Springs after a six-year absence and announces that she is about to publish a memoir dredging up a pivotal and tragic event in the family's history—a wound they don't want reopened. "Leaves you feeling both moved and gratifyingly sated." –*NY Times.* "A genuine pleasure." –*NY Post.* [2M, 3W] ISBN: 978-0-8222-2605-5

★ **TRIBES by Nina Raine.** Billy was born deaf into a hearing family and adapts brilliantly to his family's unconventional ways, but it's not until he meets Sylvia, a young woman on the brink of deafness, that he finally understands what it means to be understood. "A smart, lively play." –*NY Times.* "[A] bright and boldly provocative drama." –*Associated Press.* [3M, 2W] ISBN: 978-0-8222-2751-9

DRAMATISTS PLAY SERVICE, INC.
440 Park Avenue South, New York, NY 10016 212-683-8960 Fax 212-213-1539
postmaster@dramatists.com   www.dramatists.com

NEW PLAYS

★ **BENGAL TIGER AT THE BAGHDAD ZOO by Rajiv Joseph.** The lives of two American Marines and an Iraqi translator are forever changed by an encounter with a quick-witted tiger who haunts the streets of war-torn Baghdad. "[A] boldly imagined, harrowing and surprisingly funny drama." *–NY Times.* "Tragic yet darkly comic and highly imaginative." *–CurtainUp.* [5M, 2W] ISBN: 978-0-8222-2565-2

★ **THE PITMEN PAINTERS by Lee Hall, inspired by a book by William Feaver.** Based on the triumphant true story, a group of British miners discover a new way to express themselves and unexpectedly become art-world sensations. "Excitingly ambiguous, in-the-moment theater." *–NY Times.* "Heartfelt, moving and deeply politicized." *–Chicago Tribune.* [5M, 2W] ISBN: 978-0-8222-2507-2

★ **RELATIVELY SPEAKING by Ethan Coen, Elaine May and Woody Allen.** In TALKING CURE, Ethan Coen uncovers the sort of insanity that can only come from family. Elaine May explores the hilarity of passing in GEORGE IS DEAD. In HONEYMOON MOTEL, Woody Allen invites you to the sort of wedding day you won't forget. "Firecracker funny." *–NY Times.* "A rollicking good time." *–New Yorker.* [8M, 7W] ISBN: 978-0-8222-2394-8

★ **SONS OF THE PROPHET by Stephen Karam.** If to live is to suffer, then Joseph Douaihy is more alive than most. With unexplained chronic pain and the fate of his reeling family on his shoulders, Joseph's health, sanity, and insurance premium are on the line. "Explosively funny." *–NY Times.* "At once deep, deft and beautifully made." *–New Yorker.* [5M, 3W] ISBN: 978-0-8222-2597-3

★ **THE MOUNTAINTOP by Katori Hall.** A gripping reimagination of events the night before the assassination of the civil rights leader Dr. Martin Luther King, Jr. "An ominous electricity crackles through the opening moments." *–NY Times.* "[A] thrilling, wild, provocative flight of magical realism." *–Associated Press.* "Crackles with theatricality and a humanity more moving than sainthood." *–NY Newsday.* [1M, 1W] ISBN: 978-0-8222-2603-1

★ **ALL NEW PEOPLE by Zach Braff.** Charlie is 35, heartbroken, and just wants some time away from the rest of the world. Long Beach Island seems to be the perfect escape until his solitude is interrupted by a motley parade of misfits who show up and change his plans. "Consistently and sometimes sensationally funny." *–NY Times.* "A morbidly funny play about the trendy new existential condition of being young, adorable, and miserable." *–Variety.* [2M, 2W] ISBN: 978-0-8222-2562-1

DRAMATISTS PLAY SERVICE, INC.
440 Park Avenue South, New York, NY 10016 212-683-8960 Fax 212-213-1539
postmaster@dramatists.com www.dramatists.com

NEW PLAYS

★ **THE PICTURE OF DORIAN GRAY by Roberto Aguirre-Sacasa, based on the novel by Oscar Wilde.** Preternaturally handsome Dorian Gray has his portrait painted by his college classmate Basil Hallwood. When their mutual friend Henry Wotton offers to include it in a show, Dorian makes a fateful wish—that his portrait should grow old instead of him—and strikes an unspeakable bargain with the devil. [5M, 2W] ISBN: 978-0-8222-2590-4

★ **THE LYONS by Nicky Silver.** As Ben Lyons lies dying, it becomes clear that he and his wife have been at war for many years, and his impending demise has brought no relief. When they're joined by their children all efforts at a sentimental goodbye to the dying patriarch are soon abandoned. "Hilariously frank, clear-sighted, compassionate and forgiving." *–NY Times.* "Mordant, dark and rich." *–Associated Press.* [3M, 3W] ISBN: 978-0-8222-2659-8

★ **STANDING ON CEREMONY by Mo Gaffney, Jordan Harrison, Moisés Kaufman, Neil LaBute, Wendy MacLeod, José Rivera, Paul Rudnick, and Doug Wright, conceived by Brian Shnipper.** Witty, warm and occasionally wacky, these plays are vows to the blessings of equality, the universal challenges of relationships and the often hilarious power of love. "CEREMONY puts a human face on a hot-button issue and delivers laughter and tears rather than propaganda." *–BackStage.* [3M, 3W] ISBN: 978-0-8222-2654-3

★ **ONE ARM by Moisés Kaufman, based on the short story and screenplay by Tennessee Williams.** Ollie joins the Navy and becomes the lightweight boxing champion of the Pacific Fleet. Soon after, he loses his arm in a car accident, and he turns to hustling to survive. "[A] fast, fierce, brutally beautiful stage adaptation." *–NY Magazine.* "A fascinatingly lurid, provocative and fatalistic piece of theater." *–Variety.* [7M, 1W] ISBN: 978-0-8222-2564-5

★ **AN ILIAD by Lisa Peterson and Denis O'Hare.** A modern-day retelling of Homer's classic. Poetry and humor, the ancient tale of the Trojan War and the modern world collide in this captivating theatrical experience. "Shocking, glorious, primal and deeply satisfying." *–Time Out NY.* "Explosive, altogether breathtaking." *–Chicago Sun-Times.* [1M] ISBN: 978-0-8222-2687-1

★ **THE COLUMNIST by David Auburn.** At the height of the Cold War, Joe Alsop is the nation's most influential journalist, beloved, feared and courted by the Washington world. But as the '60s dawn and America undergoes dizzying change, the intense political dramas Joe is embroiled in become deeply personal as well. "Intensely satisfying." *–Bloomberg News.* [5M, 2W] ISBN: 978-0-8222-2699-4

DRAMATISTS PLAY SERVICE, INC.
440 Park Avenue South, New York, NY 10016 212-683-8960 Fax 212-213-1539
postmaster@dramatists.com www.dramatists.com

NEW PLAYS

★ **MOTHERHOOD OUT LOUD by Leslie Ayvazian, Brooke Berman, David Cale, Jessica Goldberg, Beth Henley, Lameece Issaq, Claire LaZebnik, Lisa Loomer, Michele Lowe, Marco Pennette, Theresa Rebeck, Luanne Rice, Annie Weisman and Cheryl L. West, conceived by Susan R. Rose and Joan Stein.** When entrusting the subject of motherhood to such a dazzling collection of celebrated American writers, what results is a joyous, moving, hilarious, and altogether thrilling theatrical event. "Never fails to strike both the funny bone and the heart." –*BackStage.* "Packed with wisdom, laughter, and plenty of wry surprises." –*TheaterMania.* [1M, 3W] ISBN: 978-0-8222-2589-8

★ **COCK by Mike Bartlett.** When John takes a break from his boyfriend, he accidentally meets the girl of his dreams. Filled with guilt and indecision, he decides there is only one way to straighten this out. "[A] brilliant and blackly hilarious feat of provocation." –*Independent.* "A smart, prickly and rewarding view of sexual and emotional confusion." –*Evening Standard.* [3M, 1W] ISBN: 978-0-8222-2766-3

★ **F. Scott Fitzgerald's THE GREAT GATSBY adapted for the stage by Simon Levy.** Jay Gatsby, a self-made millionaire, passionately pursues the elusive Daisy Buchanan. Nick Carraway, a young newcomer to Long Island, is drawn into their world of obsession, greed and danger. "Levy's combination of narration, dialogue and action delivers most of what is best in the novel." –*Seattle Post-Intelligencer.* "A beautifully crafted interpretation of the 1925 novel which defined the Jazz Age." –*London Free Press.* [5M, 4W] ISBN: 978-0-8222-2727-4

★ **LONELY, I'M NOT by Paul Weitz.** At an age when most people are discovering what they want to do with their lives, Porter has been married and divorced, earned seven figures as a corporate "ninja," and had a nervous breakdown. It's been four years since he's had a job or a date, and he's decided to give life another shot. "Critic's pick!" –*NY Times.* "An enjoyable ride." –*NY Daily News.* [3M, 3W] ISBN: 978-0-8222-2734-2

★ **ASUNCION by Jesse Eisenberg.** Edgar and Vinny are not racist. In fact, Edgar maintains a blog condemning American imperialism, and Vinny is three-quarters into a Ph.D. in Black Studies. When Asuncion becomes their new roommate, the boys have a perfect opportunity to demonstrate how open-minded they truly are. "Mr. Eisenberg writes lively dialogue that strikes plenty of comic sparks." –*NY Times.* "An almost ridiculously enjoyable portrait of slacker trauma among would-be intellectuals." –*Newsday.* [2M, 2W] ISBN: 978-0-8222-2630-7

DRAMATISTS PLAY SERVICE, INC.
440 Park Avenue South, New York, NY 10016 212-683-8960 Fax 212-213-1539
postmaster@dramatists.com www.dramatists.com